COOKING
AROUND THE WORLD

A Mexican Cookbook for Kids

Rosemary Hankin

PowerKiDS press.
New York

Published in 2014 by The Rosen Publishing Group
29 East 21st Street, New York, NY 10010

Produced for Rosen by Calcium Creative Ltd
Editor for Calcium Creative Ltd: Sarah Eason
US Editor: Sara Howell
Designer: Paul Myerscough

Picture credits: Cover: Shutterstock: Jacek Chabraszewski. Inside: Dreamstime: Pablo Caridad 9t, Crispi 9b, Uli Danner 13b, Jerl71 13t, Jeffrey Kreulen 5tl, Lunamarina 4, 5tr, Per Olsson 5b, Arturo Osorno 21t, Pipa100 7l, Jaime Leonardo Gonzalez Salazar 17b, Yurchyk 7r; Shutterstock: Azucar 25t, Bonchan 18, Joe Gough 10, Holbox 21b, Katie Smith Photography 25b, Nayashkova Olga 14, Ruth Peterkin 17t, Lori Sparkia 22, Nathalie Speliers Ufermann 26, Wavebreakmedia 6. Tudor Photography: 11, 15, 19, 23, 27.

Library of Congress Cataloging-in-Publication Data

Hankin, Rosemary.
 A Mexican cookbook for kids / by Rosemary Hankin.
     pages cm — (Cooking around the world)
 includes index.
 ISBN 978-1-4777-1334-1 (library binding) — ISBN 978-1-4777-1516-1 (pbk.) —
 ISBN 978-1-4777-1517-8 (6-pack)
 1. Cooking, Mexican—Juvenile literature. I. Title.
 TX716.M4H358 2014
 641.5972—dc23
                                        2012047948

Manufactured in the United States of America

CPSIA Compliance Information: Batch #S13PK8: For Further Information contact Rosen Publishing, New York, New York at 1-800-237-9932

Contents

Exciting Mexico

Mexico is a country that is found just south of the United States. Mexico is exciting and colorful. It has high mountains and pretty, sandy beaches. Mexico has an amazingly dramatic landscape that includes hot **deserts**, **tropical forests**, and even active **volcanoes**.

The people of this dramatic country love to cook exciting food. Mexican food as we know it today started with the **Mayans**, who were one of the first people to live in Mexico. The Mayans invented corn tortillas, which they ate with bean paste. Next came the **Aztecs**, who added chilies, honey, salt, and **cocoa** to the Mexican diet.

When the Spanish came to Mexico in 1521, they brought milk, cheese, garlic, herbs, and **spices**. Today, Mexican food includes recipes from all over the world, from the Caribbean to Africa.

Some parts of Mexico have amazing rock formations.

Mexicans love to party! Their **festivals** are full of bright, fun, colorful decorations, such as these piñatas.

Hot and flavorsome chilies are used in many Mexican dishes.

Get Set to Cook

Cooking is fun! There is nothing better than making food and then sharing it with your family and friends.

Every recipe page in this book starts with a "You Will Need" list. This is a set of **ingredients**. Be sure to collect everything on the list before you start cooking.

Look out for the "Top Tips" boxes. These have great tips to help you cook.

"Be Safe!" boxes warn you when you need to be extra careful.

Use one cutting board for meat and fish and a different cutting board for vegetables and fruit.

Always ask a grown-up if you can do some cooking.

Be sure to wash your hands before you start cooking.

Watch out for sharp knives! Ask a grown-up to help you with chopping and slicing.

Always wash any fruit and vegetables before using them.

Wear an apron to keep your clothes clean as you cook.

Always ask a grown-up for help when cooking on the stove or using the oven.

Southern Surprises

Southern Mexicans love chicken dishes such as kebabs, rice dishes, stews, and soups. They cook with lots of onion and garlic. Also on the menu are tangy vegetables, flavored with chili and spices such as cinnamon, oregano, and cilantro. Mexicans eat these dishes as a main course or as a side dish.

Everyday Meals

Tortillas are loved by Mexican people and are eaten almost every day. In the state of Oaxaca they are served with a special sauce called mole, which is made with different ingredients including bananas and peanut butter. Rich chocolate drinks are often served in Oaxaca, and the Mexicans here love cocoa so much they use it in **savory** dishes!

Insect Delights

Grasshoppers live only in some states of Mexico, including Oaxaca, and here they are eaten! *Chapulines* are grasshoppers fried with garlic, chili, and onions until they are crisp. They are served with lime juice.

Southern Mexico is full of wonders, including the Mayan ruins at Tulum.

Chapulines are eaten as a crispy snack or a tasty **taco** filling.

9

Chicken Enchiladas

olive oil
2 skinless, boneless chicken
   breast fillets, cubed
½ onion, chopped
½ cup sour cream
4 ounces (100 g) Monterey
   Jack cheese, grated
1 tsp dried parsley
pinch of dried oregano
pinch of ground black pepper
½ cup plain tomato sauce
4 tbsp water
1 tsp chili powder
1 garlic clove, crushed
3 corn tortillas
¼ cup prepared
   enchilada sauce
fresh parsley,
   chopped

Wrapping food in corn tortillas dates back thousands of years to Mayan times. Garlic, chili, and oregano are popular flavorings that are used in lots of Mexican food, including this delicious dish.

BE SAFE!
• Ask a grown-up to help you chop the chicken and onion.
• Be careful when you **sauté** on the stove.

10

STEP 1

Preheat the oven to 350°F (180°C). In a nonstick pan, sauté the chicken in olive oil until the meat is no longer pink and the juices run clear.

STEP 2

Stir in the chopped onion, sour cream, just over half the cheese, the parsley, oregano, and pepper. Heat through until the cheese melts. Stir in the tomato sauce, water, chili powder, and crushed garlic.

STEP 3

Spoon equal amounts of the chicken mixture on to each tortilla. Roll them up carefully and arrange in a baking dish. Spoon the enchilada sauce across the top. Scatter the remaining cheese over.

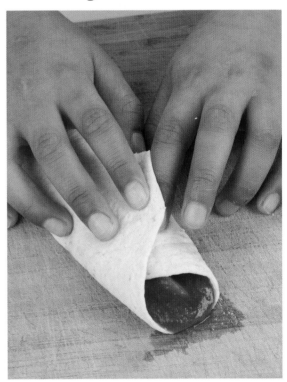

STEP 4

Place the dish in the oven and bake uncovered for 20 minutes. Cool for 10 minutes before serving, then **garnish** with fresh, chopped parsley.

TOP TIP Why not add some chopped green bell pepper in step 2? Tasty!

The Valley of Mexico

The Valley of Mexico is in central Mexico. In 1821, Mexico became independent of Spain. To celebrate, the Mexicans in the city of Puebla, in the Valley of Mexico, held a huge feast. The **nuns** of the city made a delicious new dish for the feast, which used all the colors of the Mexican flag, green, white, and red. The delicious dish is called *chile en nogada.*

Sweet and Spicy

To make chile en nogada, large poblano peppers are stuffed with lots of cooked meats and dried fruit such as raisins and dates. The peppers are then fried. Next, a creamy walnut sauce is poured over the peppers and they are decorated with pomegranate seeds.

Big and Bustling

Central Mexico is the busiest and most modern part of the country. In the capital, Mexico City, Mexicans love to eat meat such as beef, pork, goat, lamb, and mutton. *Birria* is a slow-cooked dish of goat or mutton with dried, roasted peppers. It is served with soup and tacos. Sausages are popular in central Mexico, especially chorizos. These spicy sausages are served fresh or smoked with chilies.

Many Mexican buildings are painted in pretty, bright colors. This is the city of Guanajuato in central Mexico.

Mexicans love to eat sausages in all shapes and sizes! They are made in long strings and sold in local markets.

Chili Beef Tortillas

YOU WILL NEED:

olive oil
1 onion, chopped
1 garlic clove, crushed
1 pound (450 g) ground beef
14 ounce (400 g) can chopped tomatoes
14 ounce (400 g) can kidney beans, drained
8 ounce (220 g) can corn kernels
1 red bell pepper, seeded and chopped
1 tsp chili powder
1 tsp paprika
salt, to taste
½ cup water
12 flour tortillas
Monterey Jack cheese, grated
fresh parsley

Chili beef is a great Mexican dish. It used to be made with chopped beef, but is now usually made with ground beef. There are many recipes for chili beef. This one is spicy, but not too hot!

BE SAFE!
• Ask a grown-up to help you chop the vegetables.
• Always wear oven mitts when using the oven.

STEP 1

Heat a little olive oil in a large pan. Then sauté the onion and garlic, stirring until soft. Add the ground beef and cook until browned. Stir occasionally.

STEP 2

Add the other ingredients, excluding the tortillas, cheese, and parsley. Put the lid on the pan, turn down the heat, and cook the chili beef for 30 minutes at a simmer. Stir every now and then to stop the beef from sticking to the pan. Preheat the oven to 350°F (180°C).

STEP 3

Place the tortillas in a stack and wrap them in foil. This will stop them from drying out. Place them in the oven and cook for 15 minutes.

STEP 4

Wearing oven mitts, take the tortillas out of the oven and remove the foil. Fill the tortillas with the chili beef and grated cheese, then wrap them. Garnish with parsley.

TOP TIP To make your chili beef super-spicy, add 1 tsp cayenne pepper and a little more chili powder!

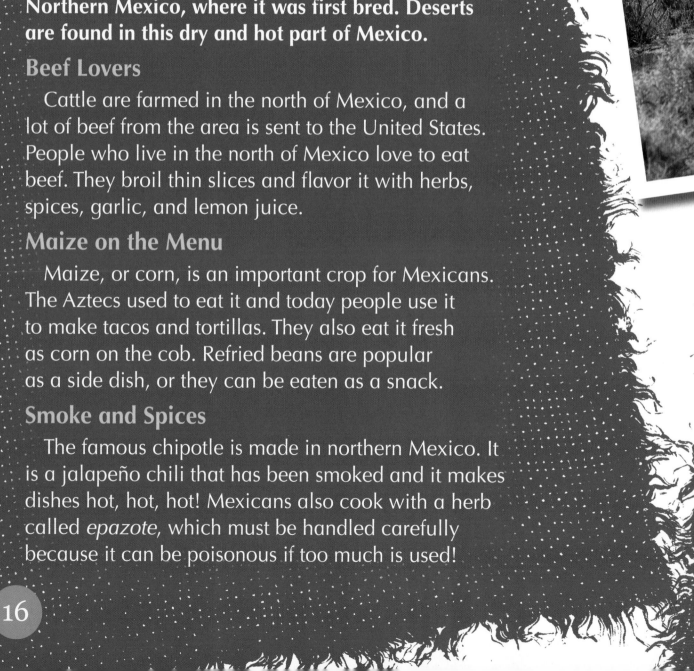

Near the Border

Have you heard of a Chihuahua dog? This cute little dog is named for the state of Chihuahua in Northern Mexico, where it was first bred. Deserts are found in this dry and hot part of Mexico.

Beef Lovers

Cattle are farmed in the north of Mexico, and a lot of beef from the area is sent to the United States. People who live in the north of Mexico love to eat beef. They broil thin slices and flavor it with herbs, spices, garlic, and lemon juice.

Maize on the Menu

Maize, or corn, is an important crop for Mexicans. The Aztecs used to eat it and today people use it to make tacos and tortillas. They also eat it fresh as corn on the cob. Refried beans are popular as a side dish, or they can be eaten as a snack.

Smoke and Spices

The famous chipotle is made in northern Mexico. It is a jalapeño chili that has been smoked and it makes dishes hot, hot, hot! Mexicans also cook with a herb called *epazote*, which must be handled carefully because it can be poisonous if too much is used!

Cactus plants grow in the Mexican desert near to the United States border.

Corn is used for many delicious dishes and also for fun decorations. Corn kernels are dyed bright colors and sold in outdoor markets in northern Mexico.

Guacamole

YOU WILL NEED:

4 mild chilies, chopped
2 fresh tomatoes, chopped
1 white onion, chopped
pinch of salt
juice of ½ lime
3 ripe avocados
fresh parsley

The Aztecs first made tasty guacamole hundreds of years ago. When the Spanish came to Mexico, they loved the dish and it is now popular all over the world!

BE SAFE!
• Never rub your eyes when handling chilies. They will really sting!
• Ask a grown-up to prepare the avocados.

18

STEP 1

Place the chilies, tomatoes, onion, and salt in a food processor. Blend until the mixture forms a smooth paste. Add the lime juice and blend again to mix.

TOP TIP If the mixture in the food processor is too stiff, add a little water.

STEP 2

Using a sharp knife, cut the avocados in half lengthways. Then separate the two halves. Remove the pit and scoop out the flesh using a spoon. Place in a mixing bowl.

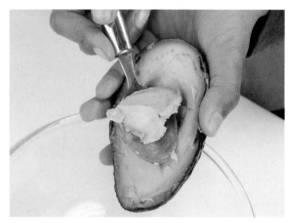

STEP 3

Mash the avocado flesh with a fork. Don't mash it for too long. You need to leave a few lumps for some texture. Add the tomato mixture and stir into the avocado until mixed.

STEP 4

Transfer the guacamole to a serving dish and garnish with fresh parsley leaves. Serve with some tortilla chips or corn chips.

Pacific Side

The western coastline of Mexico is very long. The land is beautiful, with cliffs, rocks, and great beaches. Although the sea is quite rough, fishermen go out every day to catch the many fish and shellfish found in the ocean there. Each seaside state, from Guerrero in the south to Baja California in the north, has its own special fish dishes.

Fish Flavors

Ceviche is a raw fish dish. The fish is "cooked" in lemon or lime juice. It is then flavored with onion, garlic, chili, and spicy cilantro. Ceviche is served with lettuce, corn, or avocado. Mexicans also bake fish, cook it in stews and soups, and eat it in tacos.

Cooking with Meat

Meat is also eaten in seaside parts of Mexico. The state of Sinaloa has a dish called *chilorio*, which is pork cooked with chili, garlic, oregano, and vinegar or lime juice. It is served as a filling for tacos.

Mexican fishermen also fish from the beach using huge nets. These fishermen have made a good catch!

Shrimp have been added to this ceviche. The dish has lots of sharp, tangy flavors.

Tomato Salsa

The Spanish word "salsa" means "sauce." You could try this delicious mixture with Chili Beef Tortillas, on pages 14 and 15. Salsa can be eaten cooked or uncooked. Either way, it has quite a kick!

YOU WILL NEED:

2 tbsp corn oil, plus extra for brushing
2 fresh chilies
1 small red onion, chopped
4 garlic cloves, peeled
6 fresh tomatoes, halved and seeded
salt and ground black pepper
juice of 2 limes
¼ cup fresh cilantro, chopped

BE SAFE!
• Be careful when you sauté and use the stove.
• Ask a grown-up to broil the tomatoes for you.

STEP 1

Preheat the broiler to high. Heat the corn oil in a small sauté pan and then sauté the chilies, red onion, and garlic until the mixture is soft.

STEP 2

Brush the tomatoes with corn oil. Season well with salt and ground black pepper. Broil the tomatoes on both sides until slightly **charred** and soft.

STEP 3

Place the tomatoes and the chili mixture in a food processor. Add the lime juice and blend until the mixture is smooth. Add the chopped cilantro and blend briefly again, or pulse a few times.

STEP 4

Taste a little of the salsa. You can add more salt and ground black pepper, if you wish. Then spoon the tomato salsa into a serving dish. Serve your salsa as a delicious dip with corn chips or homemade tortilla chips.

TOP TIP For fresh, uncooked salsa, finely chop the vegetables. Mix them with the lime juice, cilantro, and **seasoning**.

23

Ancient Ways

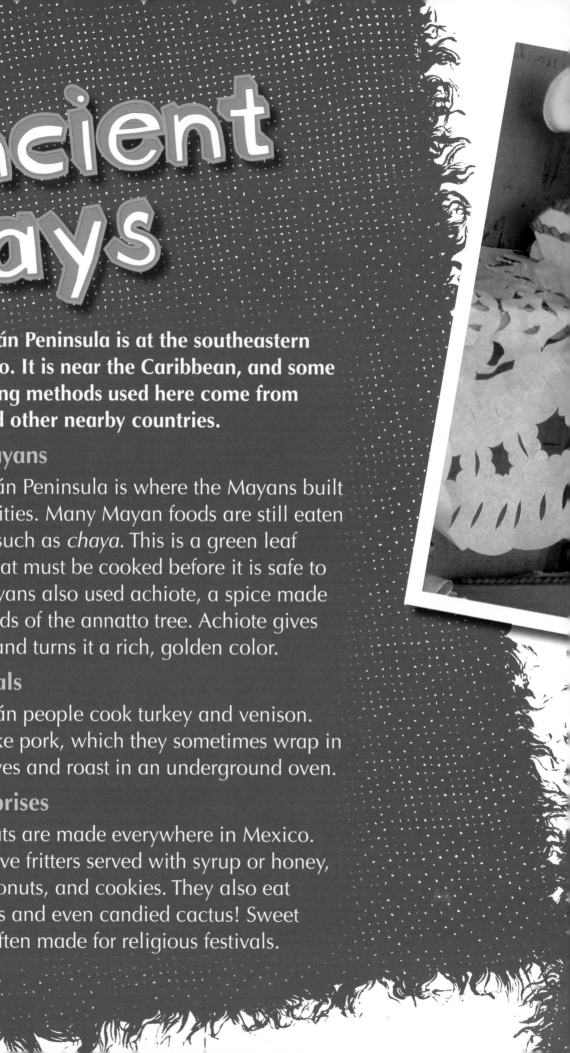

The Yucatán Peninsula is at the southeastern tip of Mexico. It is near the Caribbean, and some of the cooking methods used here come from Jamaica and other nearby countries.

Mighty Mayans

The Yucatán Peninsula is where the Mayans built their great cities. Many Mayan foods are still eaten here today, such as *chaya*. This is a green leaf vegetable that must be cooked before it is safe to eat. The Mayans also used achiote, a spice made from the seeds of the annatto tree. Achiote gives food flavor and turns it a rich, golden color.

Meaty Meals

The Yucatán people cook turkey and venison. They also like pork, which they sometimes wrap in banana leaves and roast in an underground oven.

Sweet Surprises

Sweet treats are made everywhere in Mexico. Mexicans love fritters served with syrup or honey, fruit-filled donuts, and cookies. They also eat candied nuts and even candied cactus! Sweet dishes are often made for religious festivals.

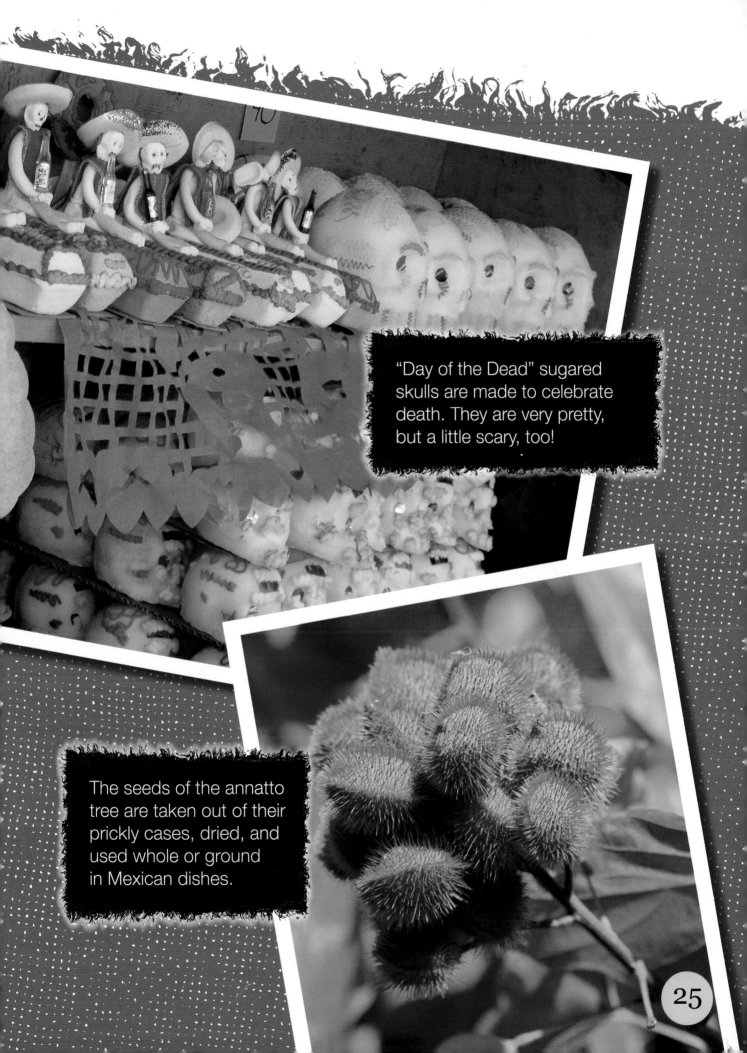

"Day of the Dead" sugared skulls are made to celebrate death. They are very pretty, but a little scary, too!

The seeds of the annatto tree are taken out of their prickly cases, dried, and used whole or ground in Mexican dishes.

Day of the Dead Bread

YOU WILL NEED:

6 cups flour
½ cup sugar
1 tsp salt
1 tbsp anise seed
2 packets dry yeast
½ cup milk
½ cup water
1 stick (½ cup) butter
4 eggs
confectioner's sugar,
  for sprinkling
2 tbsp orange
  juice

"Day of the Dead" is a festival day during which Mexicans believe they are visited by the spirits of their dead relatives. Delicious food is eaten, such as this sugared bread which is decorated with bones!

BE SAFE!
• Ask a grown-up for help with this recipe.
• Be careful when you are using the stove and oven.

STEP 1

Mix 1½ cups of flour, the sugar, salt, anise, and yeast in a large bowl. Heat the milk, water, and butter in a pan.

STEP 2

Beat the milk mixture into the flour mixture. Add the eggs and mix well. Slowly add the rest of the flour.

STEP 3

Knead the mixture on a floured surface for 10 minutes. Place in a greased bowl and leave to rise until doubled in size.

STEP 4

Shape the dough into loaves. Make "bones" from some of the dough and use it to decorate the loaves. Place them on a baking sheet and leave to rise for 1 hour. Preheat the oven to 350°F (180°C).

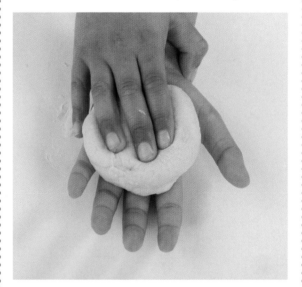

STEP 5

Bake your loaves for around 20–30 minutes. After baking, brush some orange juice over the loaves and sprinkle them with the sugar. Leave to cool.

TOP TIP Why not sprinkle your loaves with colored sugar for a pretty finish?

27

Mexican Meals on the Map!

Chihuahua

Gulf of California

Baja California

Tomato Salsa

Chili Beef Tortillas

Now that you have discovered how to cook the delicious foods of Mexico, find out where they are cooked and eaten on this map of the country.

Guacamole

United States

Gulf of Mexico

Day of the Dead Bread

Mexico

The Yucatán Peninsula

Caribbean Sea

MEXICO CITY

Guerrero   Oaxaca

Chicken Enchiladas

PACIFIC OCEAN

29

Glossary

Aztecs (AZ-teks) People who created a great empire in Mexico hundreds of years ago.

charred (CHARD) Slightly blackened from heat.

cocoa (KOH-koh) A powder that is made from cocoa pods and used to flavor food.

deserts (DEH-zurtz) Areas that have almost no rain and so have nearly no plants.

enchilada (en-chih-LAH-duh) A corn tortilla wrapped around a mix of savory ingredients and covered with sauce.

festivals (FES-tih-vulz) Large celebrations in which many people take part.

garnish (GAR-nish) To decorate food before serving.

ingredients (in-GREE-dee-untz) Different foods and seasonings that are used to make a recipe.

kebabs (kuh-BAHBZ) A meal of roasted meat cooked on skewers and eaten with bread.

Mayans (MY-inz) People who lived in the Yucatán area thousands of years ago.

nuns (NUNZ) Women who serve God all their lives.

sauté (saw-TAY) To lightly fry food in oil or butter.

savory (SAY-vuh-ree) Food that is not sweet in taste.

seasoning (SEE-zun-ing) Salt, pepper, and other herbs and spices that give food certain flavors.

spices (SPYS-ez) Powders that are rich in taste and which are used to add flavor to food.

taco (TAH-koh) A fried tortilla folded around ingredients such as meat and cheese.

tropical forests (TRAH-puh-kul FOR-ests) Forests with a very high rainfall.

volcanoes (vol-KAY-nohz) Openings in the Earth's crust from which lava flows.

Further Reading

Landau, Elaine. *Mexico*. A True Book. Danbury, CT:
    Children's Press, 2009.

Pearce, Kevin. *Foods of Mexico*. Culture in the Kitchen.
    New York: Gareth Stevens, 2012.

Ward, Karen. *Fun with Mexican Cooking*. Let's Get Cooking!.
    New York: PowerKids Press, 2010.

Websites

Due to the changing nature of Internet links, PowerKids
Press has developed an online list of websites related to
the subject of this book. This site is updated regularly.
Please use this link to access the list:
www.powerkidslinks.com/caw/mexi

Index